Porpoises
For Kids

Amazing Animal Books
For Young Readers

By
Rachel Smith

Mendon Cottage Books
JD-Biz Corp Publishing

Read More Amazing Animal Books

Purchase at Amazon.com

Table of Contents

Introduction

The porpoise, a relation of the dolphin, is a beautiful creature. It swims gracefully, much more than many humans, and is known to be fairly intelligent, like their cousin the dolphin.

Belonging to the same family as whales as well, the porpoise does not get that big in comparison. It is like a small whale in many ways.

Porpoises are also known as mereswine, which is from the French name for them, which basically means 'sea pig.' It's from distorted French that we get the name Porpoise.

In this book, you will discover the differences between the seven kinds of porpoise, and the ways it differs from whales and dolphins.

What is a porpoise?

A porpoise is, as mentioned before, a relation of whales and dolphins; this means it comes from the order Cetacea, specifically in the family Phocoenidae. The order Cetacea includes many mammals that live in the ocean exclusively.

A harbor porpoise.

It is more closely related to the dolphin than the whale, but there are several differences between the dolphin and the porpoise: first, the porpoise's beak is shorter and more rounded. Secondly, they have flat, spade-shaped teeth, whereas the dolphin has conical teeth. They are also smaller and stouter than dolphins. Other than that, there are few differences.

A porpoise relies on a certain amount of blubber (which is basically fat) to stay warm, just like dolphins and whales. Whales are often hunted for this blubber, but porpoises don't have quite the same issue, since they are much smaller.

Porpoises are predators. Unlike, say, a killer whale, which hunts things such as seals, porpoises hunt small creatures, such as fish and crustaceans. They fill themselves on this food, which also helps to keep them warm. Porpoises depend on eating frequently to keep body heat.

It depends on where they live, but typically, water makes mammals cold because it leeches the heat from them. For example, humans can get very sick if they stay in water too long, especially if it's cold water. This is called hypothermia, which means that the body isn't warm enough because the heat has been taken from it.

However, porpoises do not have this problem. Like any animal, they can starve to death, or even succumb to very cold temperatures, but they do not have the same risks being in the water that humans do.

The longest a porpoise is known to get is about 2.5 meters. The shortest tend to be closer to 1.5 meters. They are the smallest kind of cetacean. Most cetaceans depend on their fat stores (blubber) to keep them warm, but not the porpoise.

Porpoises have babies more quickly than dolphins. A porpoise carries its young for about 11 months, and they are generally single calves. Twins are incredibly unlikely with this animal, and especially anything beyond that number. They are not like dogs and cats that have litters of young.

Some types of porpoise can go up to 55 kilometers an hour! Dall's porpoise is said to be the fastest cetacean. Also, porpoises in general can dive up to 200 kilometers, but they prefer shallow waters. They can also use echolocation, sort of like a bat, to find food.

What kinds of porpoises are there?

There are considered to be about six kinds. Some say seven, but we will stick with the main six that have long been the kinds of porpoises recognized by science.

Two Dall's porpoises making 'rooster tails,' which is a kind of splash pattern they sometimes make while swimming.

First off, the most well-known is probably the harbor porpoise, which bears more resemblance to a dolphin than some others. Its color is gray, and like all porpoises, it has a rounded sort of snout, rather than a long beak like the dolphin. It would be easiest to mix up this porpoise with a dolphin if you didn't see its face.

Dall's porpoise is also a more well-known sort; it tends to remind people a little of an orca, because it is also black and white.

The finless porpoise is one that doesn't have a fin on top of its body like the other porpoises. It encompasses either three subspecies or two kinds of porpoise (scientists can't quite agree).

Fourth is the vacquita, a North American porpoise that is the smallest cetacean. It's hard to spot, unlike the first two mentioned, and there aren't as many pictures or videos of it as its cousins.

Fifth is the spectacled porpoise. This kind is black on top and white on its belly; it's far rarer than the vacquita. We don't know as much about this one as we do some of the others. They are fairly small as well.

Lastly, there's the Burmeister's porpoise, also known as the black porpoise due to its dark coloring. It has been hunted for a long time, and it's fairly unique due to the placement of its dorsal fin.

Those are the only living kinds; there are several that died out long before humans were around.

Where do porpoises live?

Porpoises live throughout the world. They live in saltwater for the most part, but some kinds of finless porpoises live in freshwater.

Top fin of a vacquita.

More than one kind lives near South America, particularly around Patagonia and the Falkland Islands. Another place is in the North, near Europe and North America.

Basically, a porpoise can live almost anywhere it's not too cold or hot for its body. Harbor porpoises can live further north than other kinds; many finless porpoises can only take going as far north as Southern Japan.

Porpoises do not live long on land; like beached whales, they will die if they don't get back in the water.

The history of porpoises and humans

Humans and porpoises have not exactly gotten along, and there are a few reasons for this.

A stamp from 1985 in the Netherlands, showing both a picture of a porpoise and a graph of how many there are at the time.

For one thing, porpoises were previously hunted for their blubber. Not as much anymore, of course, and most hunters were far more eager to go after whales, since they have far more blubber, but porpoise hunting was still a problem.

What the big problem now has become is a common problem for dolphins as well: mass fishing. Trawlers will lower their nets and drag them along, catching not only the fish they wanted to catch, but all manner of things. This includes porpoises and dolphins, who often die in these nets.

Another reason that humans have not been as kind to porpoises is that they don't do well in zoos and aquaparks, and are not nearly as trainable as their cousins the dolphins. Where dolphins can be taught to do tricks and learn to live in small enclosures, porpoises simply cannot.

There are very few porpoises in zoos and the like. It's probably for the best.

Harbor porpoise

The harbor porpoise is the best known in the Western world, especially in Europe. It lives more in a Northward direction than most of the other porpoises, and is pretty widespread, along the coasts of the Mediterranean and North America, for just two of the places it inhabits.

A harbor porpoise relaxing in the water.

It bears resemblance to a dolphin, but as with all porpoises, its snout is rounded and not a beak.

This kind of porpoise differs depending on where they live; North African harbor porpoises are different from the ones in the Black Sea, and so on. This type of porpoise lives in places such as the California coast and other parts of the Pacific Ocean, but also in the Atlantic, as far North as Iceland and Greenland. Harbor porpoises have been known to swim up rivers as well, and have been found many kilometers inland.

The females are generally heavier than the males. They also are some of the smaller porpoises, though most porpoises tend to be fairly small compared to their cetacean relatives.

Harbor porpoises prefer places such as fjords, harbors, and other sheltered areas. This is where they get their name.

They also eat fish that swim in groups, such as herring and sprat. They will dive fairly deep to get at them, though sprat tend to be more towards the surface; this type of fish, the harbor porpoise will stay near the surface to hunt. They generally hunt alone, but on rare occasions the harbor porpoise will hunt in a group.

Harbor porpoises generally like to stay in the same area. However, they will move about in search of food. They are known as sedentary, meaning that they stay in the same place. Many humans could be considered sedentary, since many of us stay in the same place.

This type of porpoise can dive over 200 meters. They usually only dive for about a minute, but they can dive for five minutes at least.

Males will mate with any female they can. Females can have babies by the time they are three or four years old; in fact, the harbor porpoise can nurse one baby and grow another at the same time. Human mothers can't do this.

Once, long ago, this type of porpoise was hunted for both food and its blubber. Back in the 19th and early 20th centuries, for example, the blubber was used as fuel for lamps. These lamps were called oil lamps, and were the reason for many cetaceans' deaths. Nowadays, oil is gotten in a different way.

Nowadays, this kind of porpoise is really only hunted by the Greenlanders, who need it to survive.

Harbor porpoises are not endangered. There are hundreds of thousands of them throughout the world. However, certain populations may be in danger of being forced out of their home or into a sort of extinction.

The harbor porpoise is protected in most places by a number of agreements between nations. There is not a likelihood that this animal will disappear from our oceans any time soon.

Vacquita

A vacquita (also spelled vaquita) is the smallest kind of porpoise. Its name means "little cow" in Spanish. It's also called cochito, desert porpoise, and gulf porpoise. Sometimes, due to the fact it lives in the Bay of California, it's also called the California Bay porpoise or some similar name.

A pair of vacquitas swimming; these animals are harder to get photographs of.

There are possibly less than 100 left. The vacquita is the most endangered cetacean that's still around (the previous most endangered, the baiji, was considered extinct in 2006). The vacquita is incredibly rare, and only lives in one part of the Bay of California.

It's got a stocky build, dark rings around its eyes, patches on its lips, and lines on its face. It has a distinct look to it. It also is dark gray, but it fades to a whitish color on its underside.

The vacquita is a slow-paced animal most of the time. It tends to move about at a leisurely speed, slowly getting its food and coming up to breathe. It also avoids all boats, so it is very hard to spot.

Vacquitas aren't very social. Generally, a vacquita will only spend time either with its calf (if it's a mother) or a mate during mating season, though it is not certain there is a mating season with vacquitas. They communicate through high-pitched noises, and use echolocation to find things.

They are one of the only types of porpoises that live in very warm waters. Vacquitas live generally in lagoons, known to survive in lagoons so shallow that they can't sink beneath the surface. They also eat many types of fish; a vacquita is not that picky, eating anything from squids to bony fish.

The vacquita is one of the top 100 most endangered species in the world. The suspected reason for the decline is fishing nets. Vacquitas get caught in nets cast for a type of fish whose swim bladder is a delicacy in China, and they die.

The totoaba, which is the fish they are hunting, is also endangered, and steps have been taken by the country of Mexico to save both. The United States is also taking some steps, but neither seem to be enough.

Dall's porpoise

Dall's porpoise lives in the North Pacific Ocean. It is black and white, a beautiful creature that reminds people of orcas, or killer whales. However, it is not nearly as bloodthirsty as the larger cetacean, and tends to be a gentler creature.

A Dall's porpoise.

Dall's porpoise has a unique shape: thick body, small head. It makes it stand out among its cetacean family. It also can be dark gray to black, and the top of its fin is usually sort of dusted gray or white.

This type of porpoise lives anywhere from the Bering Sea to the Sea of Japan. Like most porpoises, it does not fear cold water due to its layer of blubber. In colder weather, it often goes south to California and on the side of the Pacific, to Southern Japan. It prefers to live in deeper areas, offshore. But the Dall's porpoise does not travel too far from shore, and has been known to venture further inland.

Dall's porpoise has sexual dimorphism, which means that the sexes are different from each other in appearance. This means that the males are bigger than the females in this case.

They eat small fish, and cephalopods, such as octopuses. Sometimes they eat krill too, a tiny animal that the blue whale also eats, but the Dall's porpoise does not rely on krill in the same way the blue whale does.

The predators of this animal include killer whales or orcas and white sharks. In other ways, it is the victim of a type of fluke (which is a tiny parasite) that can cause its death; another animal that uses it for survival is the whale louse, though this one isn't nearly as deadly.

Dall's porpoises live in small groups, anywhere from two to twelve. However, when they are feeding, they are much more likely to be in large groups, which may number in the hundreds or even the thousands.

Dall's porpoises like to go fast. They are the fastest small cetacean, and can nearly go as fast as an orca. They also enjoy fast boats, and will ride along its current. They do not jump out of the water like dolphins do. A spray they make when swimming just under the surface of the water is called a "rooster tail" because the pattern resembles a rooster's tail.

When it comes to mating, a male may mate with many females. Typically, they will guard the female until they get a chance to have a calf with her; then, it is typically up to the mother to take care of the calf.

Most females can give birth every year, because gestation is about 10 to 11 months, and the nursing period is only two.

They live about fifteen years in the wild. And many make it to that age.

Dall's porpoises are doing fairly well in terms of conservation; they are not in danger of being extinct any time soon. However, considering that thousands of them are killed each year, there are concerns that they may be endangered soon. This type of porpoise is typically hunted in huge number, and back in the 1980's, as many as 40,000 were captured in one year.

That number has gone down significantly.

No agreements have been made to protect the Dall's porpoise. It is not considered to be an important animal to protect at this point.

However, outside of the numbers hunted, many Dall's porpoises end up killed by being caught in nets meant for fish, and they also often get hit by boats.

Burmeister's porpoise

Burmeister's porpoise is a South American porpoise, living off the coast of South America. It is often called marsopa espinosa, which means 'thorny porpoise' or chancho marino, which means sea-pig.

It was named by Hermann Burmeister, the first European man to describe it. He's said to have discovered it, but truthfully, the native South Americans had a name for it first.

Less is known about Burmeister's porpoise. It was once believed they were black, but this is because many of the specimens caught were already dead, and this type of porpoise turns black within minutes of death. Instead, Burmeister's porpoise is more of a gray.

It's a common enough creature in its habitat, which extends from Peru on one side of South America, all the way around the bottom tip, and up to part of Brazil.

The Burmeister's porpoise has two things about it that distinguish it from the Chilean dolphin, which lives in much of the same area. First, it has an indentation in its head, right in front of its blowhole. Next, it has a different shaped fin; it points backwards more than up, and is further back on its body than any other cetacean.

This type of porpoise is very shy. It swims away from boats and comes toward the surface as little as it can. Even when getting air, the porpoise will barely get to the surface and then go back down again.

Because it's so shy, scientists don't know very much about it. It's a mystery what the mating rituals are, though we know they eat fish such as mackerel.

Like many of its relatives, it is in trouble when it comes to nets: many are killed by being caught by accident in fish nets. This is a huge problem facing almost all porpoises and dolphins.

Spectacled porpoise

The spectacled porpoise is so named because of two rings around its eyes that look sort of like glasses. Not a lot is known about it, as is common with many South American creatures.

In fact, it was only described in scientific circles in about 1912! It's only been known for about a hundred years, at least to academic circles. One can guess that the native people of South America already knew some about it.

The species is not just spotted in South America, however; instead, it tends to be around the lowest part of the Southern hemisphere. It's been spotted near Tasmania, as well as in the Southern Indian Ocean.

Very little is known. No one has caught one alive, because they are very shy.

Finless porpoise

A finless porpoise is simply what its name says: a porpoise without a fin on top of its body. There's a bit of debate over whether or not there are two kinds of finless porpoise or one; the two names are narrow-ridged finless porpoise and Indo-Pacific finless porpoise, however, they tend to be lumped together anyway.

A finless porpoise.

However, in other opinions, there are three subspecies that live in different areas: from the Persian gulf to Taiwan, the Yangtze River, and then the last subspecies from Taiwan to the East China sea and

Southern Japan. Debate is fierce on these creatures, and no consensus (agreement between people) has been reached.

They much prefer shallow water, only going out into the ocean as deep as 50 meters. That may be very deep for humans, but it isn't deep for cetaceans! In fact, this kind of porpoise has been known to live in areas more inland than the sea.

Finless porpoises have ridges on their backs instead of fins. Unlike many of their fellow porpoises, there was never a big drive to hunt them. Only just after World War II, in Japan, it was hunted because there were very few seaworthy fishing boats, but since then it is protected in Japan.

The finless porpoise is unlike other porpoises in another way: it survives in captivity. Many have been known to live up to fifteen years.

They also tend to live in groups, and depending on which kind of finless porpoise, they have groups from 2-6 porpoises big.

Conclusion

Porpoises are interesting creatures, though there is a lot more to know about them. Hopefully, in future years, we will learn a lot about these sea mammals.

And hopefully, we will find a solution for the porpoises being caught in nets. It would be a great shame to lose such a creature due to carelessness.

Author Bio

Rachel Smith is a young author who enjoys animals. Once, she had a rabbit who was very nervous, and chewed through her leash and tried to escape. She's also had several pet mice, who were the funniest little animals to watch. She lives in Ohio with her family and writes in her spare time.

Publisher

JD-Biz Corp

P O Box 374

Mendon, Utah 84325

http://www.jd-biz.com/

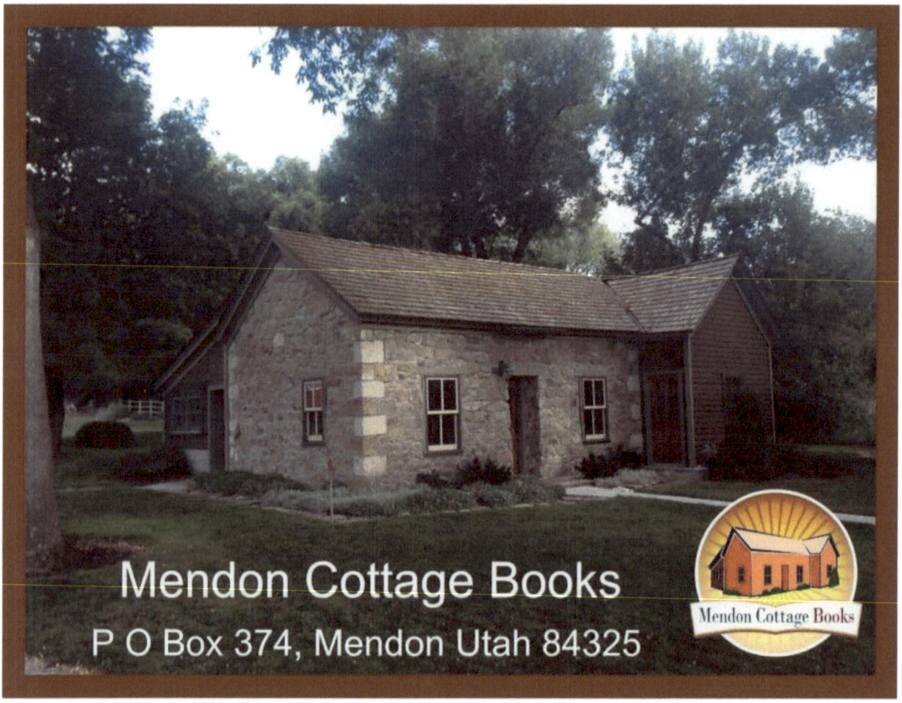

Mendon Cottage Books

P O Box 374, Mendon Utah 84325

Horses
For Kids
Amazing Animal Books
For Young Readers
By John and
Annalee Davidson

Ponies
For Kids
Mendon Cottage Books
AmazingAnimalBooks
Rachel Smith

Ten Amazing Horses
For Kids
Nature Books for Kids
JD-Biz Publishing
K. Bennett

Akhal-Teke
"The Golden Horse
of the desert"
For Kids
Nature Books for Kids
JD-Biz Publishing
K. Bennett

Suffolk Punch
"The Gentle Giant"
For Kids
Nature Books for Kids
JD-Biz Publishing
K. Bennett

Shires
"The great Horse"
For Kids
Nature Books for Kids
JD-Biz Publishing
K. Bennett

Colonial Spanish
"Horse of the Americas"
For Kids
Nature Books for Kids
JD-Biz Publishing
K. Bennett

Canadian
"The Little Iron Horse"
For Kids
Nature Books for Kids
JD-Biz Publishing
K. Bennett

Cleveland Bays
"History and Future"
Horses For Kids
Nature Books for Kids
JD-Biz Publishing
K. Bennett

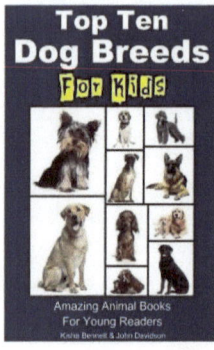

Top Ten Dog Breeds For Kids

Amazing Animal Books For Young Readers

Kisha Bennett & John Davidson

German Shepherds

Dog Books for Kids

K. Bennett

Bulldogs

Dog Books for Kids

K. Bennett

Dachshund

Dog Books for Kids

K. Bennett

Poodles

Dog Books for Kids

K. Bennett

Labrador Retrievers

Dog Books for Kids

K. Bennett

Rottweilers

Dog Books for Kids

K. Bennett

Boxers

Dog Books for Kids

K. Bennett

Golden Retrievers

Dog Books for Kids

K. Bennett

Puppies

Dog Books For Kids

Amazing Animal Books

By John Davidson

Beagles

Dog Books for Kids

K. Bennett

Yorkshire Terriers

Dog Books for Kids

K. Bennett

Dogs

Top Ten Dog Breeds For Kids

Amazing Animal Books For Young Readers

Zahra Jazeel & John Davidson

Cats

For Kids

Amazing Animal Books For Young Readers

K. Bennett & John Davidson

Foxes

For Kids

Amazing Animal Books For Young Readers

Zahra Jazeel & John Davidson

Wolves

For Kids

Amazing Animal Books For Young Readers

By John Davidson and Virginia Fidler

www.ingramcontent.com/pod-product-compliance
Lightning Source LLC
Chambersburg PA
CBHW050908290526
45792CB00002B/747